PreTime® Piano

Popular

2010 EDITION

Primer Level

Beginning Reading

Arranged by

Nancy and Randall Faber

Production Coordinator: Jon Ophoff
Design and Illustration: Terpstra Design, San Francisco
Engraving: Dovetree Productions, Inc.

FABER
PIANO ADVENTURES®

3042 Creek Drive
Ann Arbor, Michigan 48108

A NOTE TO TEACHERS

PreTime® Piano Popular is an exciting collection of popular hits arranged for the Primer-level pianist. The selections provide excellent reinforcement of basic rhythms and note reading. The pieces are primarily in Middle C position.

Teacher duets provide vitality and color. They can be played and enjoyed by parents and older siblings as well.

PreTime® Piano Popular is part of the *PreTime® Piano* series arranged by Faber and Faber. "PreTime" designates the primer level of the *PreTime® to BigTime® Piano Supplementary Library*.

Following are the levels of the supplementary library, which lead from *PreTime®* to *BigTime®*.

PreTime® Piano	(Primer Level)
PlayTime® Piano	(Level 1)
ShowTime® Piano	(Level 2A)
ChordTime® Piano	(Level 2B)
FunTime® Piano	(Level 3A – 3B)
BigTime® Piano	(Level 4)

Each level offers books in a variety of styles, making it possible for the teacher to offer stimulating material for every student. For a complimentary detailed listing, e-mail faber@pianoadventures.com or write us at the mailing address below.

Visit **www.PianoAdventures.com.**

Helpful Hints:

1. The student should know his/her part well before attempting ensemble playing. The duet part can be used first to demonstrate the rhythmic feel or "groove" of the song, however.

2. When performed up to tempo, some of the pieces have a feeling of cut time. An effective approach to these pieces is to have the student begin with the quarter note at a moderate tempo and then work up to a fast quarter note beat. This essentially provides "built-in" slow practice, while also meeting the student's need for a sense of speed and mastery.

3. The selections appear in approximate order of difficulty.

4. The student may go through several *PreTime®* books, at the teacher's discretion, before moving up to *PlayTime® Piano* (Level 1).

ISBN 978-1-61677-042-6

TABLE OF CONTENTS

It's a Small World

from "It's a Small World"
at Disneyland Park and
Magic Kingdom Park

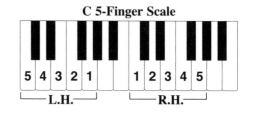

C 5-Finger Scale

Words and Music by
RICHARD M. SHERMAN
and ROBERT B. SHERMAN

Playfully

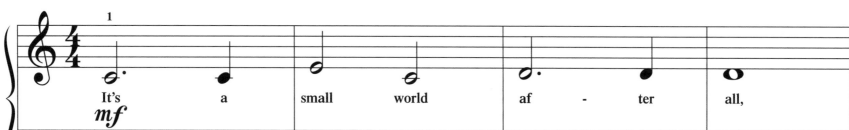

It's a small world af - ter all,

it's a small world af - ter all.

Teacher Duet: (Student plays 1 octave higher)

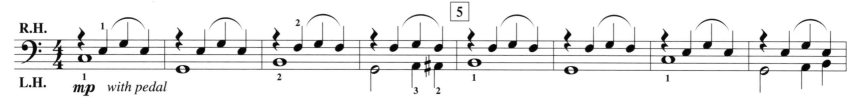

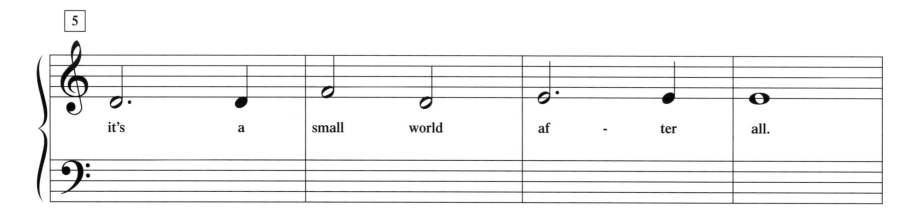

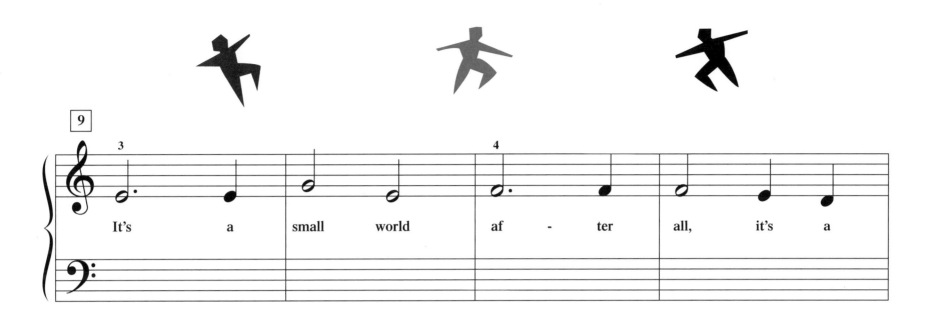

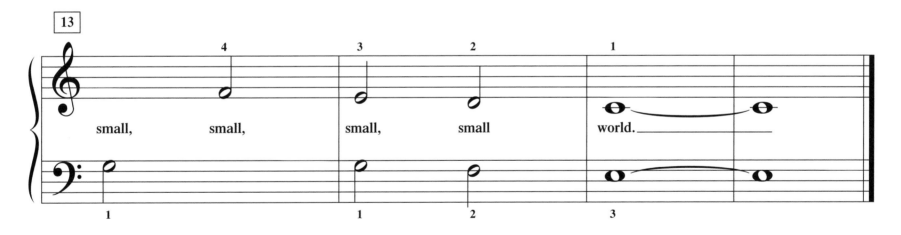

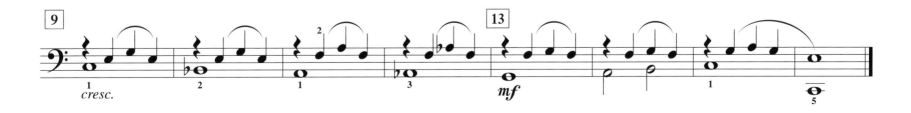

Oompa-Loompa Doompadee-Doo

from *Willy Wonka and the Chocolate Factory*

Thumbs share Middle C

Words and Music by
LESLIE BRICUSSE
and **ANTHONY NEWLEY**

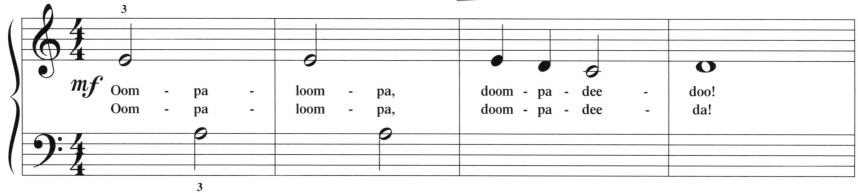

mf

Oom - pa - loom - pa, doom - pa - dee - doo!
Oom - pa - loom - pa, doom - pa - dee - da!

I've got a per - fect puz - zle for you!
If you're not greed - y, you will go far!

Teacher Duet: (Student plays 1 octave higher)

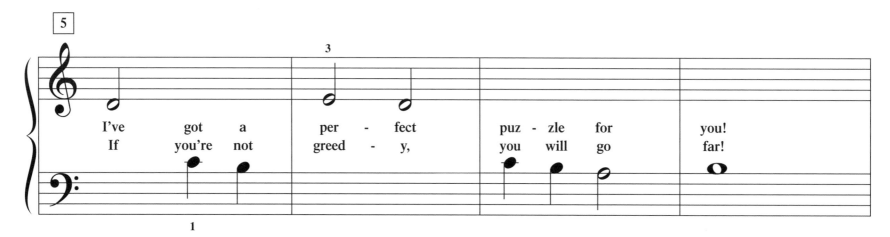

R.H.

L.H. *mp with pedal*

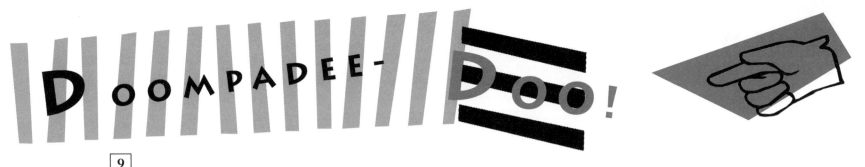

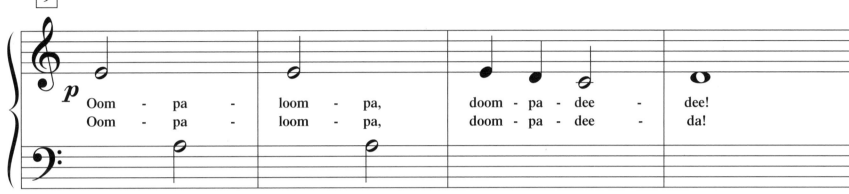

9

Oom - pa - loom - pa, doom - pa - dee - dee!
Oom - pa - loom - pa, doom - pa - dee - da!

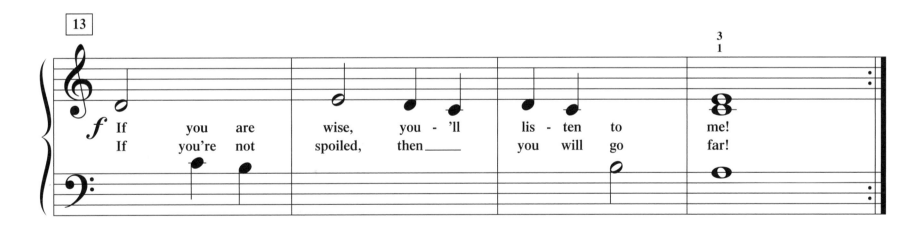

13

If you are wise, you-'ll lis - ten to me!
If you're not spoiled, then you will go far!

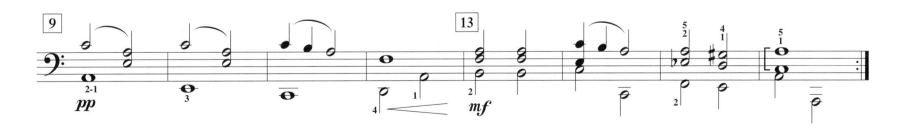

Part of Your World

from Walt Disney's *THE LITTLE MERMAID*

Music by ALAN MENKEN
Lyrics by HOWARD ASHMAN

Moderately

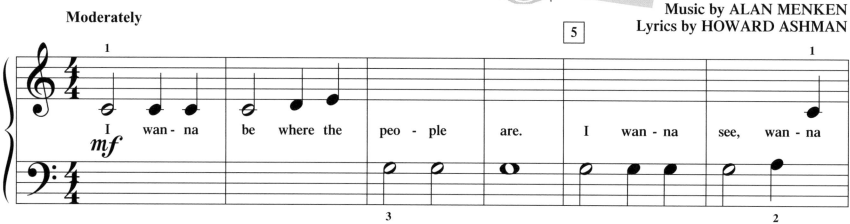

I wan - na be where the peo - ple are. I wan - na see, wan - na

see 'em dan - cin', walk - in' a - round on those what d'ya call 'em

Teacher Duet: (Student plays 1 octave higher)

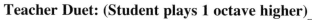
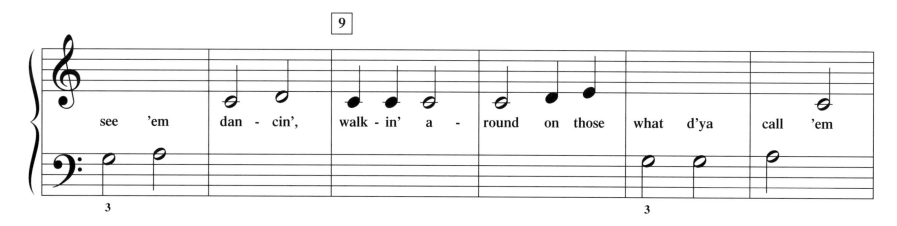

R.H.

L.H.   *with pedal*
mp

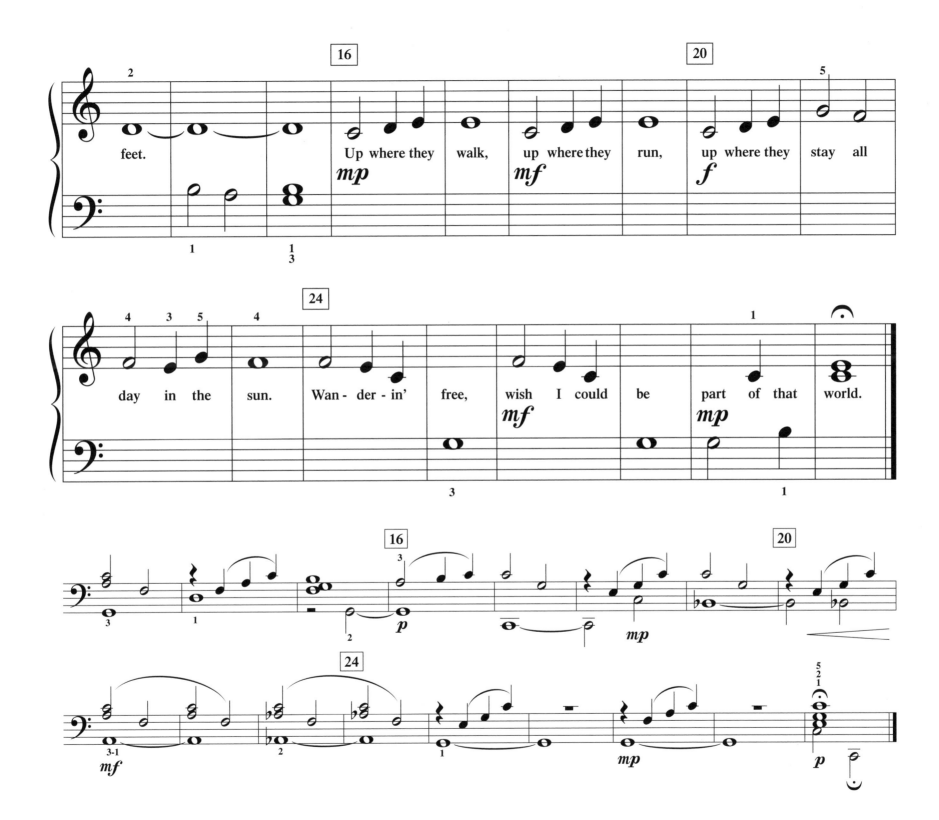

I Just Can't Wait To Be King

from Walt Disney Pictures' *THE LION KING*

Hand Position

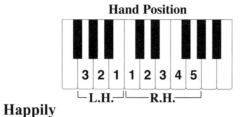

Music by ELTON JOHN
Lyrics by TIM RICE

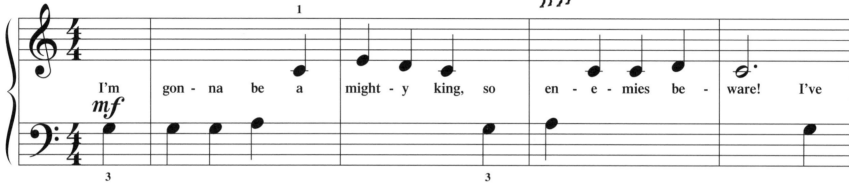

Happily

I'm gon - na be a might - y king, so en - e - mies be - ware! I've

nev - er seen a king of beasts with quite so lit - tle hair. Oh, I

Teacher Duet: (Student plays 1 octave higher)

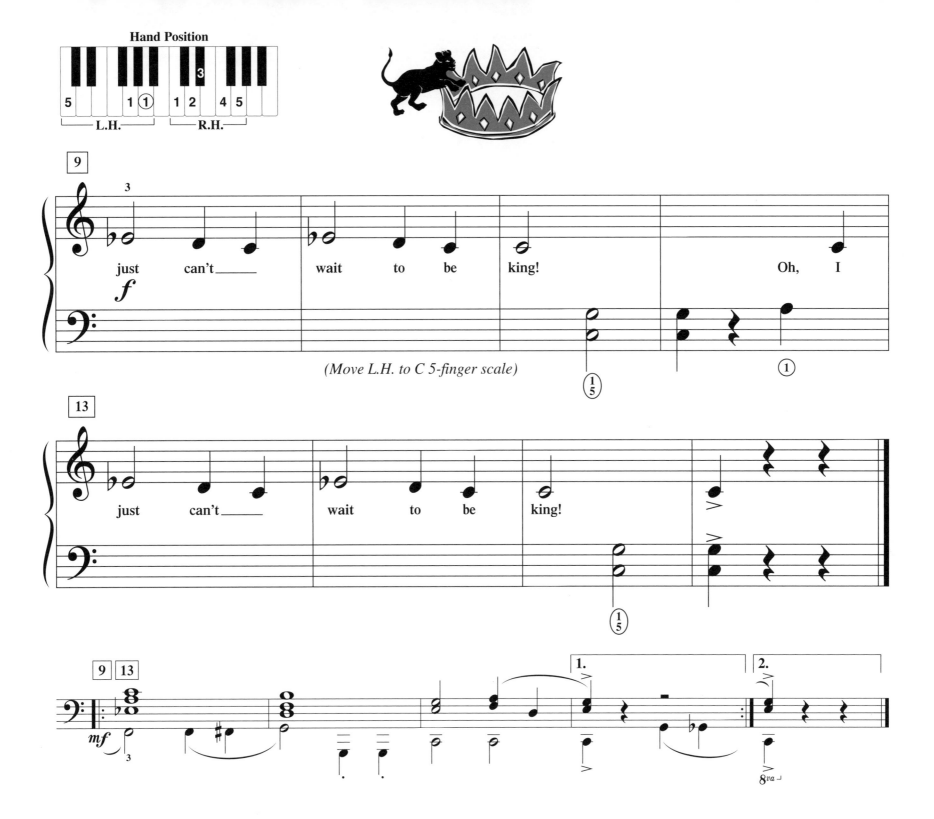

The Merry-Go-Round Broke Down

Words and Music by
CLIFF FRIEND and DAVE FRANKLIN

The merry-go-round broke down, but you don't see me frown. Things

turned out fine and now she's mine, 'cause (the) merry-go-round broke down!

Teacher Duet: (Student plays 1 octave higher)

Scooby Doo Main Title

Thumbs share Middle C

Words and Music by JOSEPH BARBERA, WILLIAM HANNA, and HOYT CURTIN

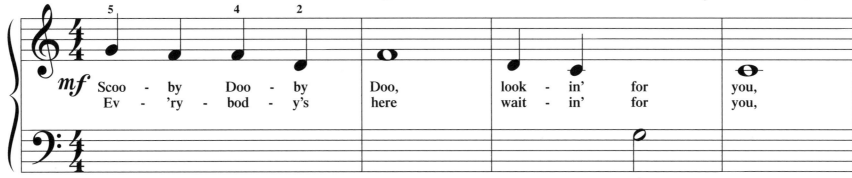

Lively

Scoo - by Doo - by Doo, look - in' for you,
Ev - 'ry - bod - y's here wait - in' for you,

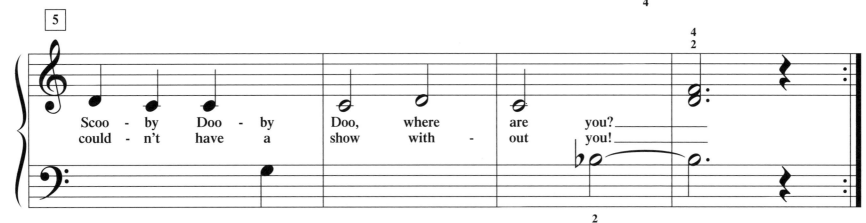

Scoo - by Doo - by Doo, where are you?
could - n't have a show with - out you!

Teacher Duet: (Student plays 1 octave higher)

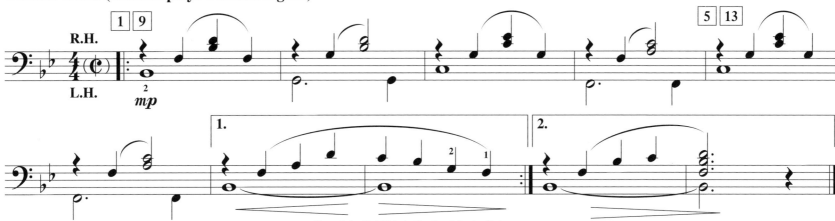

R.H.
L.H.
mp

1.
2.

If I Only Had a Brain

from *The Wizard of Oz*

Thumbs share Middle C

Music by HAROLD ARLEN
Lyrics by E.Y. HARBURG

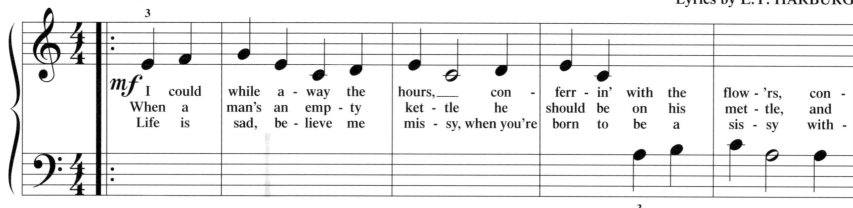

Teacher Duet: (Student plays 1 octave higher)

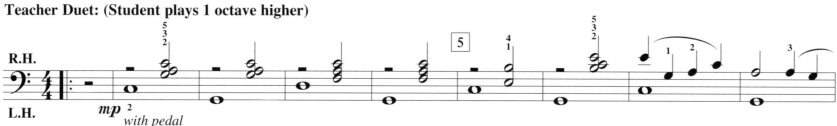

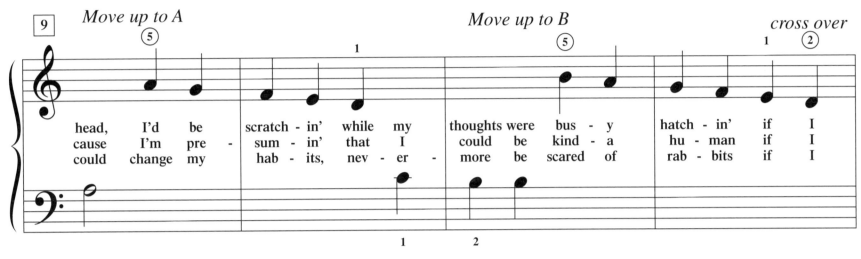

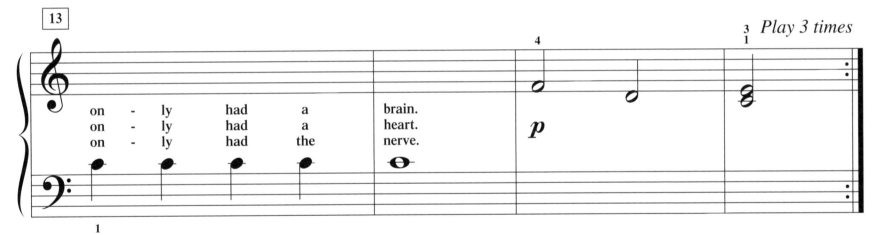

The Candy Man

from *Willy Wonka and the Chocolate Factory*

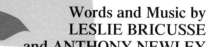

Words and Music by
LESLIE BRICUSSE
and ANTHONY NEWLEY

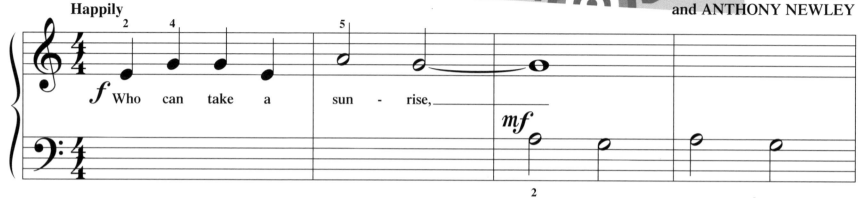

Teacher Duet: (Student plays 1 octave higher)

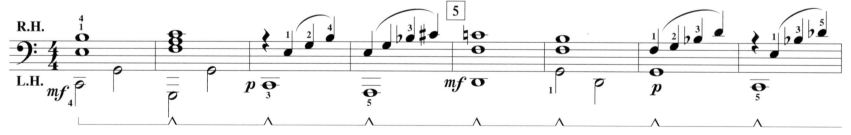

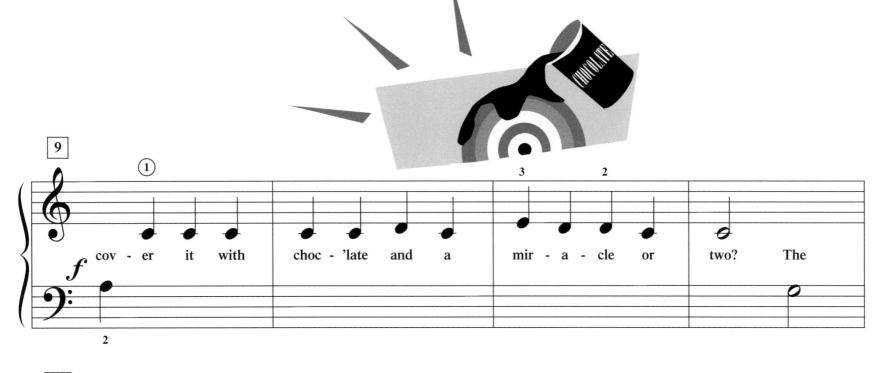

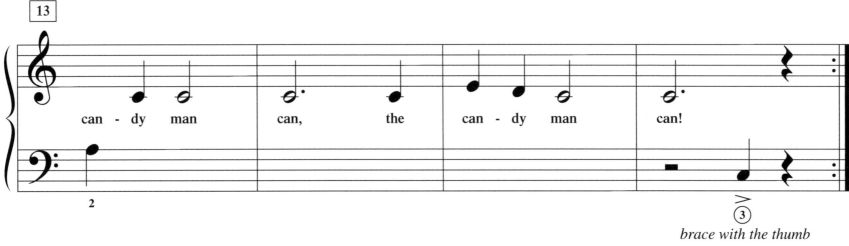

brace with the thumb

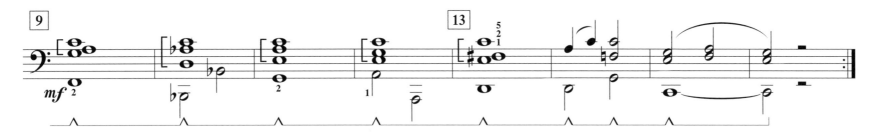

The Pirates Who Don't Do Anything

from *VeggieTales*

Words and Music by
MIKE NAWROCKI
and KURT HEINECKE

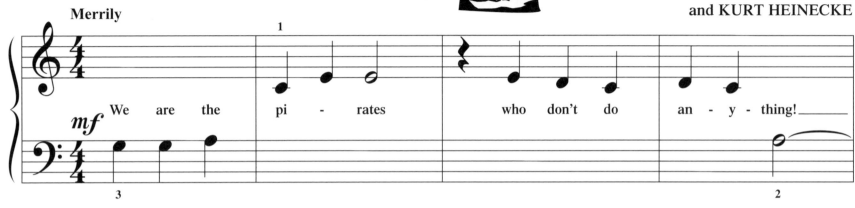

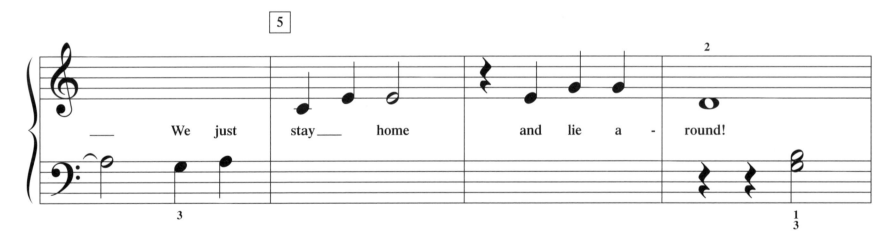

We are the pi - rates who don't do an - y - thing!____

____ We just stay____ home and lie a - round!

Teacher Duet: (Student plays 1 octave higher)

9

If you ask___ us to do an - y - thing___

13

___ we'll just tell___ you, *f* We don't do an - y - thing!

cresc.

mf

Groove Tune

By RANDALL FABER

Moving along

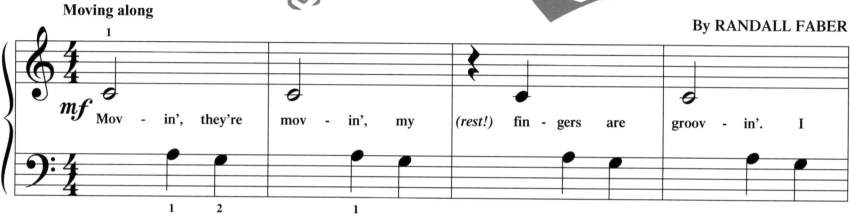

Mov - in', they're mov - in', my (*rest!*) fin - gers are groov - in'. I

love to feel the rhy - thm. Come on, let's play! (*1 - 2 - 3 - 4*)

Optional: For solo performance, the student may play *Groove Tune* three times, moving one octave lower for each repeat. Begin *forte* and play softer with each repeat.

Teacher Duet: (Student plays 1 octave higher)